37 VIOLIN PIECES
You Like to Play

WITH PIANO ACCOMPANIMENT

G. SCHIRMER, Inc.

DISTRIBUTED BY

HAL•LEONARD®
CORPORATION

7777 W. BLUEMOUND RD. P.O. BOX 13819 MILWAUKEE, WI 53213

INDEX BY COMPOSERS

Serenade.

Edited and Fingered by
PH. MITTELL.

JOSEPH HAYDN.

40130 x

Printed in the U.S.A.

For André Polah

Aurore
Aurora

Gabriel Fauré
Arranged by Arthur Hartmann (A.S.C.A.P.)

40130 c

Melody.

Edited and Fingered by
PH. MITTELL.

I. J. PADEREWSKI.

40130

L'Abeille.

(The Bee.)

Edited and Fingered by
PH. MITTELL.

FRANÇOIS SCHUBERT.

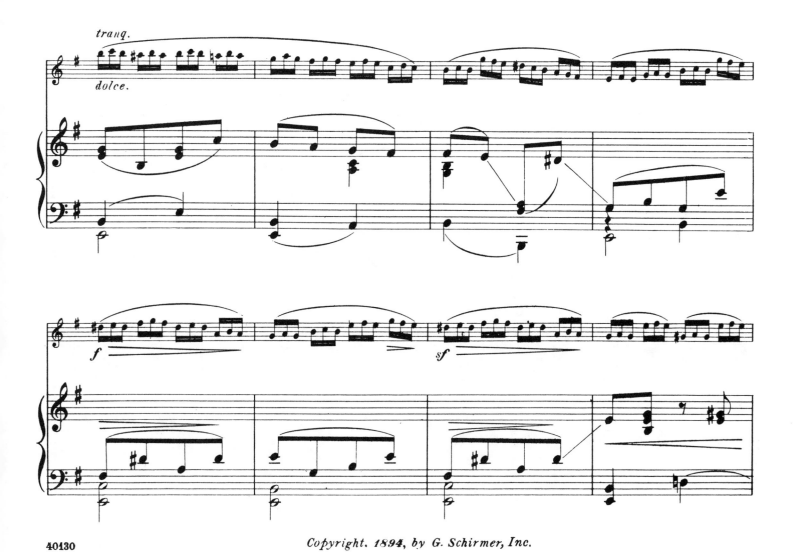

40130

Le Cygne
(The Swan)
(Extrait du Carnaval des Animaux)

Edited and Fingered by
PH. MITTELL

Camille Saint-Saëns

40130

Le Cygne
(The Swan)
(Extrait du Carnaval des Animaux)

Edited and Fingered by
PH. MITTELL

Camille Saint-Saëns

40130

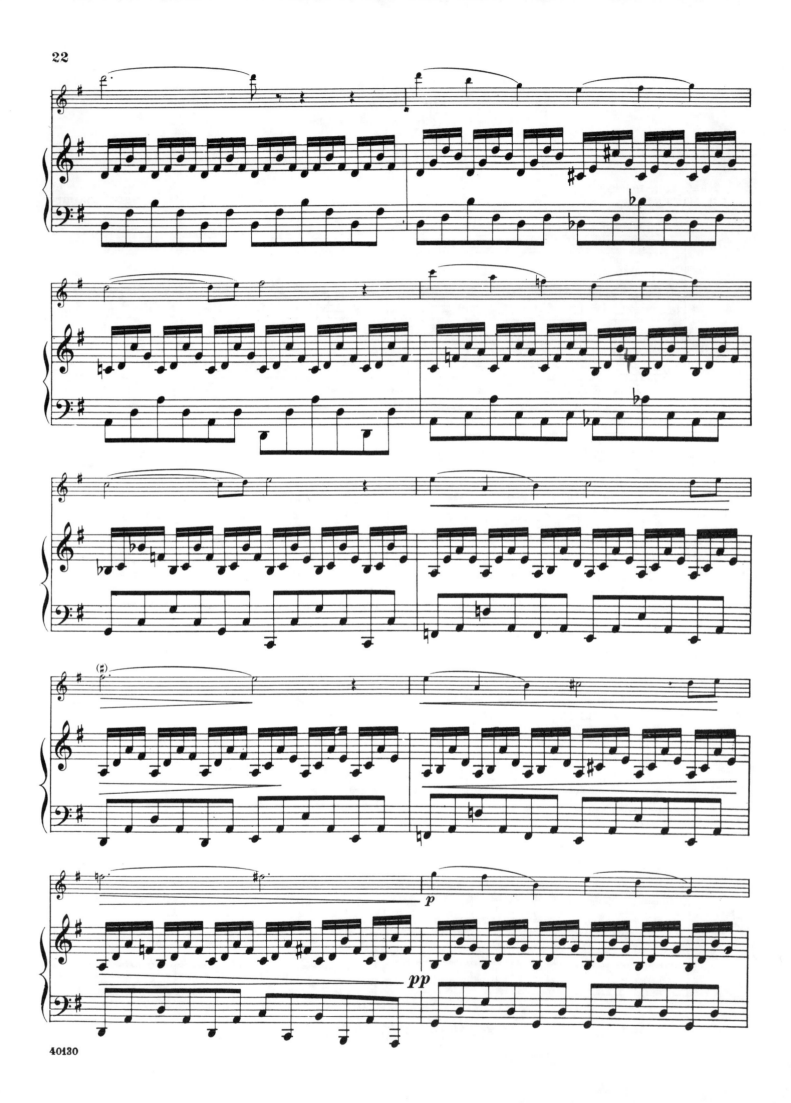

Spanischer Tanz

(Spanish Dance)

FABIAN REHFELD. Op. 58, № 1

Souvenir

Edited and fingered by Ph. Mittell

FRANZ DRDLA

40130

Valse-Bluette
Air de Ballet by R. Drigo

Transcr. by Leopold Auer

40130

Chanson

Transcribed for Violin with
Piano accompaniment by
A. Walter Kramer

Rudolf Friml

40130

Copyright, 1920, by G. Schirmer, Inc.

Largo.

Edited and fingered by
PHILIPP MITTELL.

G. F. HAN

Largo.

Edited and fingered by
PHILIPP MITTELL.

G. F. HANDEL.

Canzonetta.

VICTOR HERBERT.

Romance.

Edited and fingered by
PH. MITTELL.

JOHAN S. SVENDSEN. Op. 26.

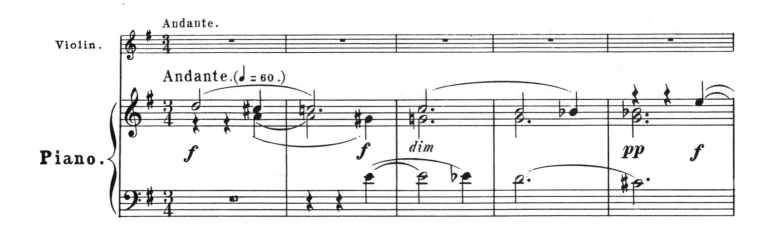

40130

Canzonetta.

from Violin-Concerto.

Peter Ilyitch Tchaikovsky, Op. 35

Belle Nuit

Barcarolle from "Contes d'Hoffman"

J. Offenbach
Transcr. by A. W. Lilienthal

40130

Serenata.

M. Moszkowski. Op. 15, № 1.
Transcribed by F. Rehfeld.

40130

Berceuse

from

"Jocelyn."

(**B. Godard.**)

Edited and fingered by
PHILIPP MITTELL.

AUTHOR'S TRANSCRIPTION!

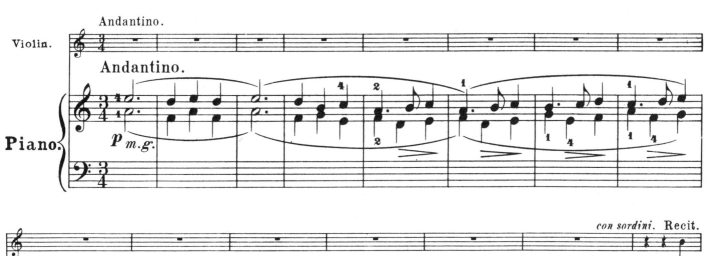

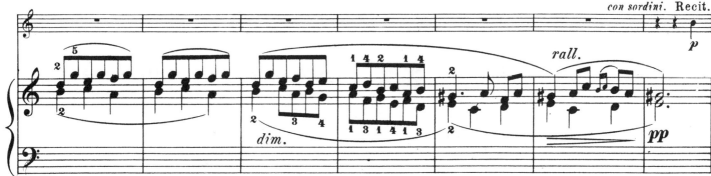

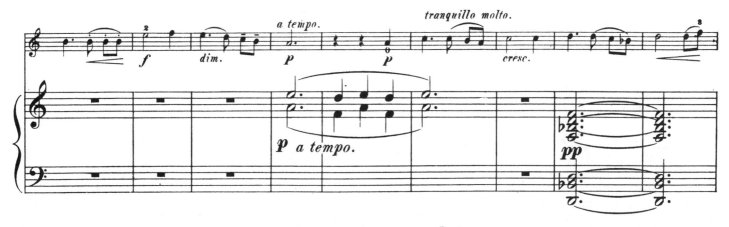

Mazurka.

Edited and fingered by
Otto K. Schill.

E. Młynarski.

40130

78

40130

40130

La Serenata.
(Angels' Serenade.)
LÉGENDE VALAQUE.
by
G. BRAGA.

Edited and Fingered by
PH. MITTELL.

Transcription by
A. POLLITZER.

40180

82

40130

La Cinquantaine

Air dans le style ancien

Edited and Fingered by
PH. MITTELL

GABRIEL - MARIE

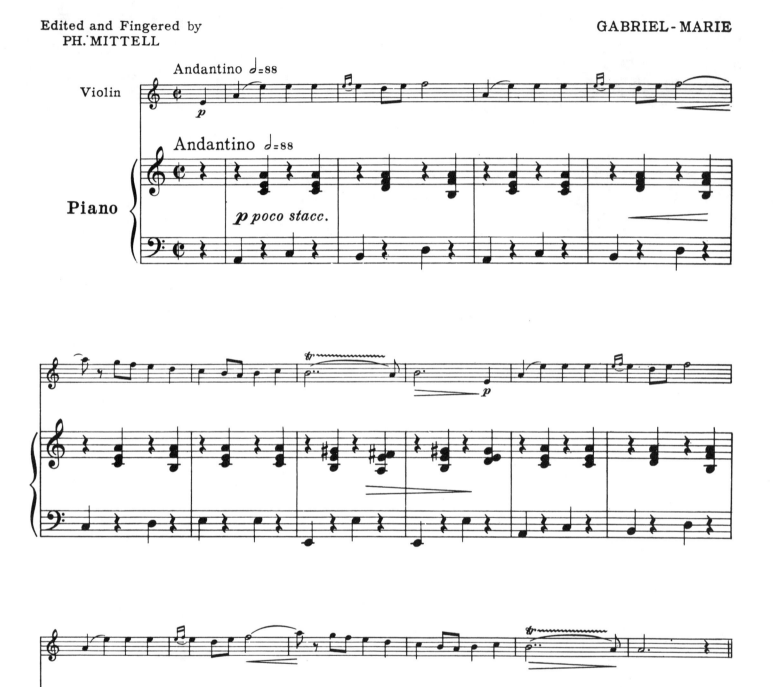

À Hugues Heermann

"Hejre Kati"
Scene from the Czárda

Revised and fingered by
Philipp Mittell

Jenö Hubay. Op.32, No.4.

Allegro moderato. (♩=100)

Träume.

(Dreams.)

Edited and fingered by
PHILIPP MITTELL

RICHARD WAGNER.

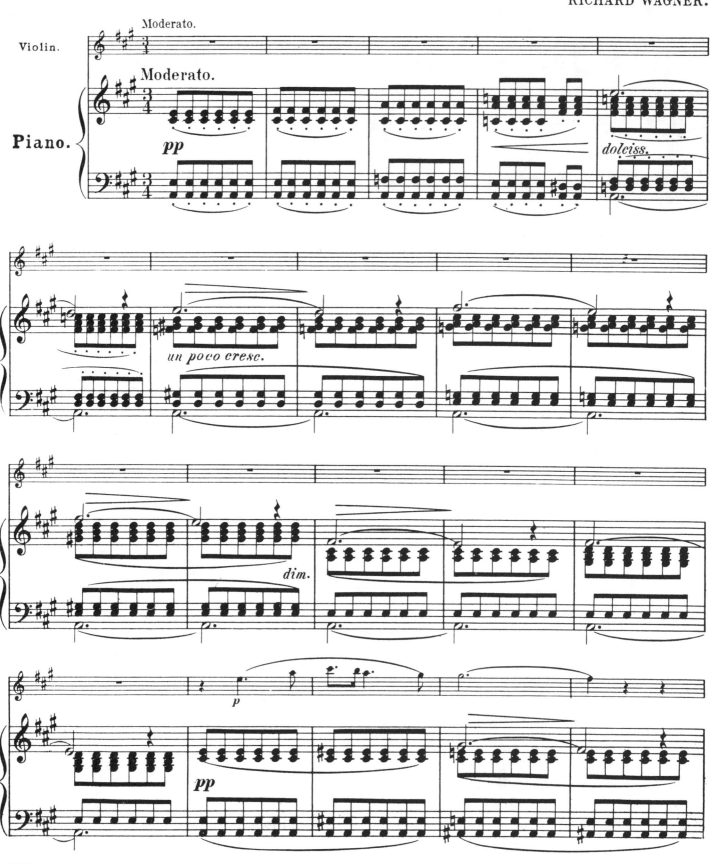

40130

Walther's Prize-Song

from

"Die Meistersinger."

(R. Wagner.)

Edited and fingered by
PHILIPP MITTELL

Paraphrase by
AUGUST WILHELMJ.

40130

Kol Nidrei.
Hebrew Melody.

110

Edited and fingered by
PHILIPP MITTELL.

MAX BRUCH. Op. 47.

40180

Copyright, 1897, by G. Schirmer, Inc.
Copyright, 1910, by G. Schirmer, Inc.

Copyright renewal assigned, 1939,
to G. Schirmer, Inc.

40130

A Eugene Gandolfo

Canzonetta

A. d' AMBROSIO. Op.6

Copyright, 1898, by Paul Decourcelle
Copyright renewal assigned, 1926, to G. Schirmer, Inc.

122

40130

Sérénade.

Edited and fingered by
PHILIPP MITTELL.

G. PIERNÉ.

40130

Romance
from
Second Concerto

fingered by
MITTELL.

HENRI WIENIAWSKI. Op. 22.

Air

by

Johann Sebastian Bach.

Arr. by AUGUST WILHELMJ.

Madrigale.

A. SIMONETTI.

The Son of the Puszta.
Hungarian.

Edited and fingered by
PHILIPP MITTELL.

KELER BÉLA. Op. 134, № 2.

Copyright renewed, 1938, by G. Schirmer, Inc.

Copyright, 1910, by G. Schirmer, Inc.

Beau Soir
Evening Fair

Claude Debussy
Arranged by Arthur Hartmann (A.S.C.A P.)

One pedal to each measure

Copyright, 1943, by G. Schirmer, Inc.
International Copyright Secured

Menuet
from
Quintet in E,
by
Luigi Boccherini.

Edited and Fingered by
PH. MITTELL.

Arr. by FR. HERMANN.

149

40130

Cradle-Song
Wiegenlied

Edited and fingered
by Philipp Mittell

Johannes Brahms. Op. 49, № 4
Arr. by Friedrich Hermann

Loin du Bal.

Edited and Fingered by
PH. MITTELL.

ERNEST GILLET.

40130

Rêverie.
Adagio for Violin and Piano.

HENRI VIEUXTEMPS. Op. 22, № 3.

40130

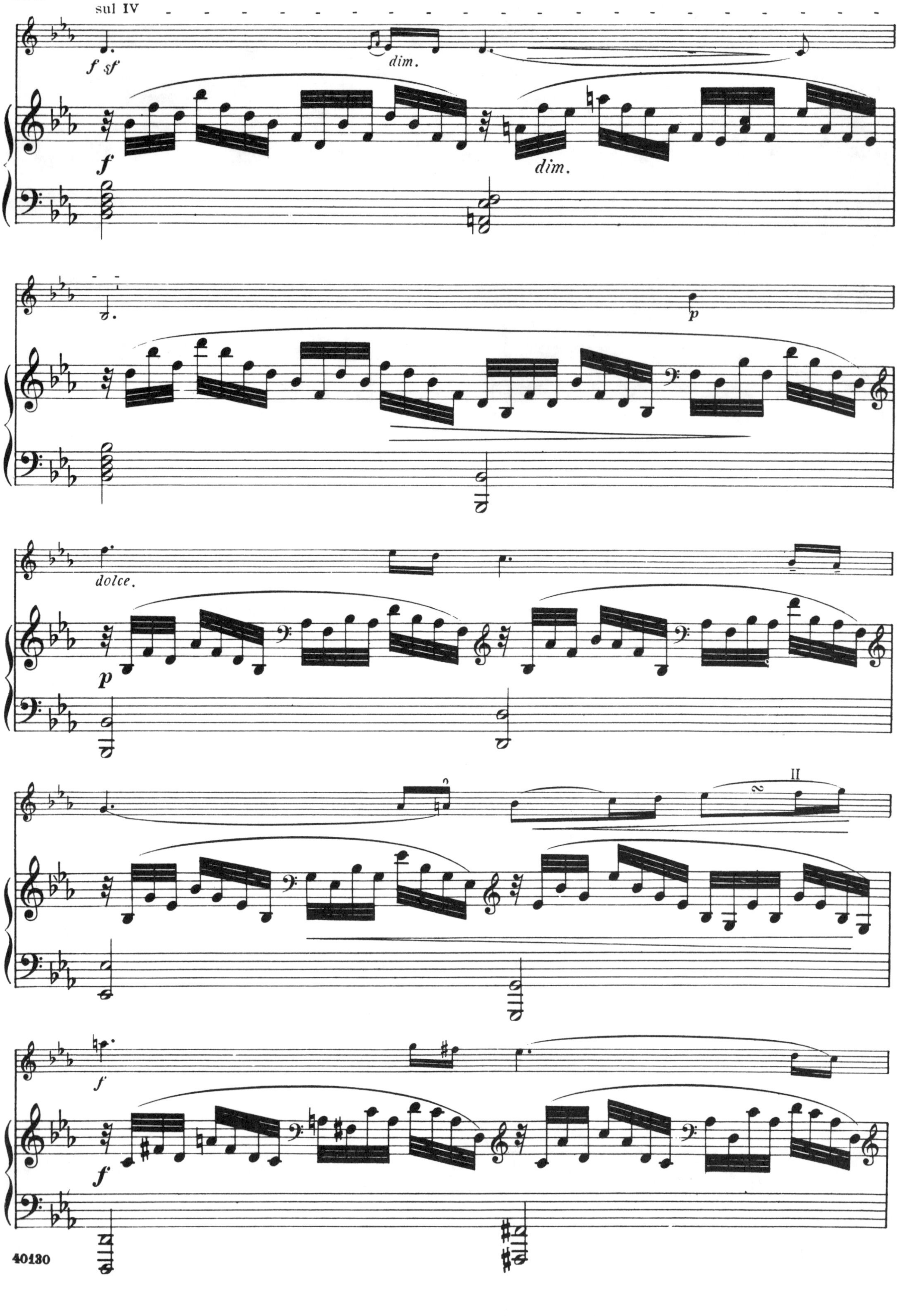
sul IV
f sf
dim.
f
dim.
p
dolce.
p
II
f
f

166

40130

Serenade
Leise flehen meine Lieder

Edited and fingered by
Paul Th. Miersch

Franz Schubert
Arranged by Hans Sitt

40130

Ave Maria

Edited by Carl Deis

Franz Schubert. Op. 52, No. 6
Arranged by August Wilhelmj

40130

colla parte

Ped.   Ped.   Ped.

Ped.   segue   Ped.   Ped.

Ped.

cresc.

Ped.   Ped.

f

fp

Ped.   Ped.   Ped.

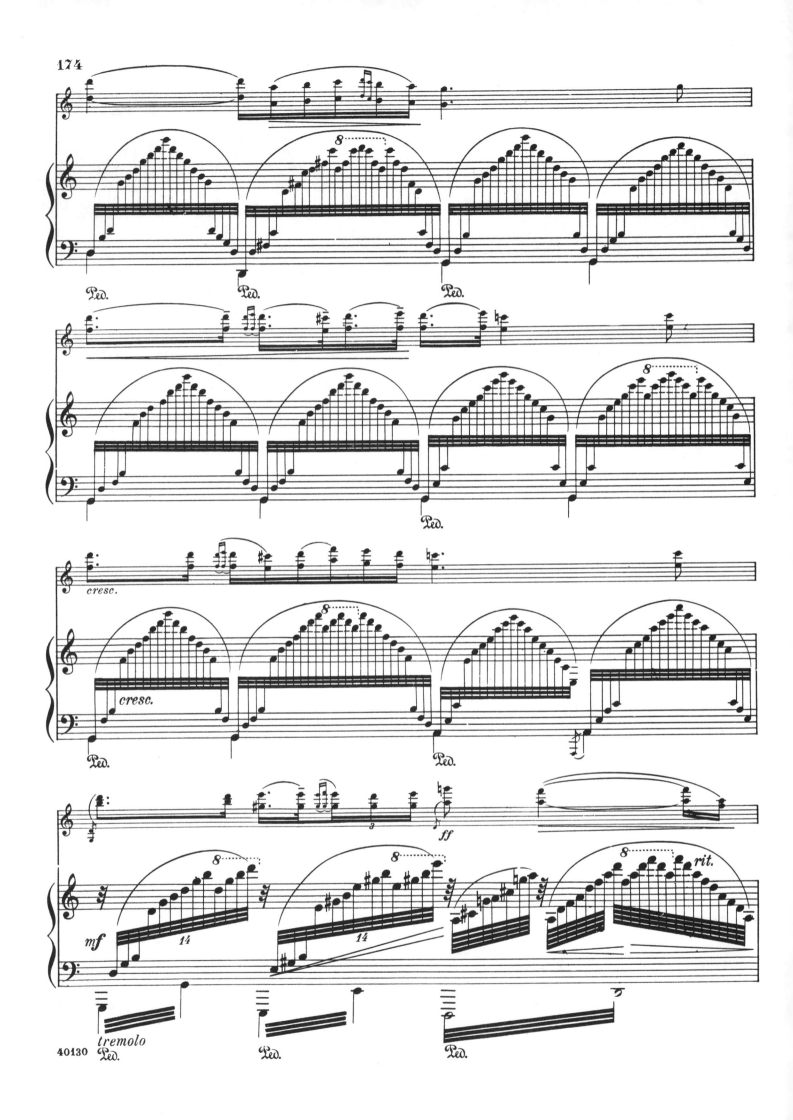

Obertass.
Mazurka.

Edited and fingered by
PHILIPP MITTELL.

H. WIENIAWSKI. Op. 19, № 1.

178

40130